WINTER WARMERS

PIES

igloobooks

igloobooks

Published in 2016
by Igloo Books Ltd
Cottage Farm
Sywell
NN6 0BJ
www.igloobooks.com

Food photography and recipe development
© Stockfood, The Food Media Agency

Cover image: © Cultura RM / Alamy Stock Photo

Cover designed by Nicholas Gage
Edited by Natalie Baker

LEO002 0916
2 4 6 8 10 9 7 5 3 1
ISBN 978-1-78670-150-3

Printed and manufactured in China

CONTENTS

MINI PIES

CHICKEN VOL-AU-VENTS

MAKES
16

PREPARATION TIME: 10 MINUTES
COOKING TIME: 15 - 20 MINUTES

450 g / 1 lb all-butter puff pastry

1 egg, beaten

3 tbsp butter

100 g / 3 ½ oz / 1 ⅓ cups button
mushrooms, sliced

1 tbsp plain (all purpose) flour

300 ml / 10 ½ fl. oz / 1 ¼ cups milk

2 tsp Dijon mustard

150 g / 5 ½ oz cooked chicken breast, chopped

METHOD

- Preheat the oven to 220°C (200°C fan) / 425F / gas 7 and line a baking tray with greaseproof baking paper.

- Roll out the pastry on a floured surface and use a 7 cm (3 in) round pastry cutter to cut out 32 circles.

- Transfer 16 circles to a baking tray and remove the centres from the rest with a 4 cm (1 ½ in) cutter.

- Attach the pastry rings to the bases with a little beaten egg then transfer the cut-out centres to the tray and brush everything with egg.

- Bake the pastry for 15–20 minutes.

- Heat half of the butter in a frying pan and fry the mushrooms for 5 minutes.

- Heat the rest of the butter in a pan and stir in the flour.

- Gradually add the milk and stir until it thickens.

- Stir in the mustard, chicken and mushrooms and season.

- Spoon the mix into the cases and top with a pastry lid.

PUFF PASTRY CHICKEN PIES

MAKES
4

PREPARATION TIME: 15 MINUTES
COOKING TIME: 45 MINUTES

2 tbsp butter

1 leek, chopped

1 carrot, chopped

1 tsp plain (all-purpose) flour

250 ml / 9 fl. oz / 1 cup milk

200 g / 7 oz cooked chicken breast, cubed

75 g / 2 ½ oz / ½ cup peas, defrosted if frozen

800 g / 1 lb 12 oz all-butter puff pastry

1 egg, beaten

METHOD

- Preheat the oven to 200°C (180°C fan) / 400F / gas 6.

- Heat the butter in a saucepan and fry the leek and carrot for 5 minutes without colouring.

- Sprinkle in the flour and stir well, then stir in the milk and bubble until it thickens slightly.

- Add the chicken and peas to the pan and heat through, then season to taste with salt and white pepper.

- Roll out the pastry on a lightly floured surface and cut out 4 circles.

- Divide the filling between 4 individual pie dishes and brush the rims with water.

- Top each pie with a pastry lid and press the edges to seal. Lightly score the pastry into a diamond pattern then brush the tops with beaten egg.

- Bake the pies for 25–30 minutes or until the pastry is golden brown and puffy.

SHORTCRUST CHICKEN PIES

MAKES
4

PREPARATION TIME: 45 MINUTES
COOKING TIME: 45 MINUTES

2 tbsp butter

1 onion, chopped

1 potato, chopped

1 tsp plain (all-purpose) flour

250 ml / 9 fl. oz / 1 cup milk

200 g / 7 oz cooked chicken breast, cubed

75 g / 2 ½ oz / ½ cup peas, defrosted if frozen

75 g / 2 ½ oz / 1 cup button mushrooms, quartered

6 cherry tomatoes, quartered

FOR THE PASTRY:

100 g / 3 ½ oz / ½ cup butter, cubed and chilled

200 g / 7 oz / 1 ⅓ cups plain (all-purpose) flour

METHOD

- First make the pastry. Rub the butter into the flour until the mixture resembles fine breadcrumbs.

- Stir in just enough cold water to bring the pastry together into a pliable dough then chill for 30 minutes. Preheat the oven to 200°C (180°C fan) / 400F / gas 6.

- Heat the butter in a saucepan and fry the onion and potato for 5 minutes without colouring. Sprinkle in the flour and stir well, then stir in the milk and bubble until it thickens slightly.

- Add the chicken, peas, mushrooms and tomatoes to the pan and heat through, then season to taste. Roll out the pastry on a floured surface and cut out 4 circles.

- Divide the filling between 4 individual pie dishes and brush the rims with water. Top each pie with a pastry lid and crimp the edges to seal.

- Bake the pies for 25–30 minutes.

LAMB, SAGE AND CORIANDER PIES

MAKES
6

PREPARATION TIME: 2 MINUTES
COOKING TIME: 1 HOUR 30 MINUTES

2 tbsp olive oil

1 small onion, finely chopped

2 cloves of garlic, crushed

½ tsp coriander (cilantro) seeds

a few sprigs of sage, tied with string

450 g/ 1 lb lamb shoulder, cubed

600 ml / 1 pint / 2 ½ cups lamb stock

FOR THE TOPPING:

450 g / 1 lb floury potatoes, peeled and cubed

100 ml / 3 ½ fl. oz / ½ cup milk

50 g / 1 ¾ oz / ¼ cup butter

50 g / 1 ¾ oz / ⅓ cup panko breadcrumbs

a few sprig of sage to garnish

METHOD

- Heat the oil in a saucepan and fry the onion, garlic, coriander seeds and sage for 3 minutes. Add the lamb shoulder and fry for 2 minutes then add the stock and bring to a gentle simmer.

- Lay a crumpled sheet of greaseproof paper on top of the meat and cover the pan with a lid then simmer very gently for 2 hours.

- Preheat the oven to 200°C (180°C fan) / 400F / gas 6.

- Cook the potatoes in salted water for 10 minutes, or until they are tender, then drain well. Return the potatoes to the saucepan and add the milk and butter, then mash until smooth.

- Remove the sage from the lamb then shed the meat with 2 forks and season to taste with salt and pepper. Arrange 6 metal ring moulds on a baking tray and half-fill each one with the lamb.

- Top the lamb with the mashed potato and sprinkle with breadcrumbs, then bake in the oven for 15 minutes or until the tops are golden brown.

- Unmould the pies onto warm plates and garnish with sage.

MINI VEGETABLE QUICHES

MAKES
4

PREPARATION TIME: 1 HOUR
COOKING TIME: 35–40 MINUTES

2 tbsp olive oil

1 small onion, finely chopped

1 large carrot, diced

1 courgette (zucchini), diced

3 large eggs

225 ml / 8 fl. oz / ¾ cup double (heavy) cream

100 g / 3 ½ oz / ½ cup butter, cubed

200 g / 7 oz / 1 ⅓ cups plain (all-purpose) flour

1 large egg, beaten

METHOD

- To make the pastry, rub the butter into the flour until the mixture resembles fine breadcrumbs.

- Stir in enough cold water to bring the pastry together into a pliable dough and chill for 30 minutes.

- Preheat the oven to 190°C (170°C fan) / 375F / gas 5.

- Roll out the pastry on a floured surface and use it to line 4 individual tart cases.

- Prick the pastry with a fork, line with greaseproof baking paper and fill with baking beans or rice.

- Bake the cases for 10 minutes then remove the paper and baking beans.

- Meanwhile, heat the oil in a frying pan and fry the onion, carrot and courgette for 5 minutes or until softened.

- Gently whisk the eggs with the cream until smoothly combined, then stir in the vegetables and season generously with salt and pepper.

- Pour the filling into the pastry cases, then lower the oven temperature to 150°C (130°C fan) / 300F / gas 2 and bake for 20 minutes or until just set in the centre.

CHERRY TOMATO AND FETA TARTS

MAKES
4

PREPARATION TIME: 10 MINUTES
COOKING TIME: 15 MINUTES

250 g / 9 oz all-butter puff pastry

100 g / 3 ½ oz feta, cubed

150 g / 5 ½ oz cherry tomatoes, halved

1 tbsp basil leaves, finely chopped

2 tbsp olive oil

METHOD

• Preheat the oven to 220°C (200°C fan) / 425F / gas 7.

• Roll out the pastry on a floured surface and cut out 4 circles.

• Transfer the pastry to a baking tray and arrange the feta and tomatoes on top.

• Mix the basil with the oil and a pinch of salt and pepper and drizzle it over the tarts.

• Bake for 15 minutes or until the pastry is cooked through.

CHOCOLATE AND BANANA MERINGUE PIES

MAKES
4

PREPARATION TIME: 55 MINUTES
COOKING TIME: 28 MINUTES

100 g / 3 ½ oz / ½ cup butter, cubed

200 g / 7 oz / 1 ⅓ cups plain
(all-purpose) flour

4 large ripe bananas

1 lime, juiced

75 g / 2 ½ oz / ½ cup dark
chocolate chips

FOR THE MERINGUE:

4 large egg whites

110 g / 4 oz / ½ cup caster
(superfine) sugar

METHOD

• Preheat the oven to 200°C (180°C fan) / 400F / gas 6.

• Rub butter into the flour and add cold water to bind. Chill for 30 minutes then roll out on a floured surface.

• Line 4 tart cases with pastry and prick the bases.

• Line the pastry with cling film and fill with baking beans or rice then bake for 10 minutes.

• Remove the cling film and beans and cook for 8 minutes.

• Mash the bananas with the lime juice until smooth then stir in half of the chocolate chips.

• Divide the mixture between the pastry cases.

• Whisk the egg whites until stiff, then gradually add the sugar and whisk until the mixture is thick and shiny.

• Spoon into a piping bag and pipe onto the tarts.

• Return the tarts to the oven to bake for 10 minutes.

• Sprinkle over the remaining chocolate chips and serve.

MINI KIWI CLAFOUTIS

MAKES
4

PREPARATION TIME: 10 MINUTES
COOKING TIME: 25 MINUTES

75 g / 2 ½ oz / ⅓ cup caster (superfine) sugar

75 g / 2 ½ oz / ⅓ cup butter

300 ml / 10 ½ fl. oz / 1 ¼ cups
whole milk

2 large eggs

50 g / 1 ¾ oz / ⅓ cup plain (all-purpose) flour

2 tbsp ground almonds

4 kiwis, cut into 4 slices

METHOD

• Preheat the oven to 190°C (170°C fan) / 375F / gas 5.

• Melt the butter in a saucepan and cook over a low heat until it starts to smell nutty.

• Brush a little of the butter around the inside of 4 gratin dishes then sprinkle with caster sugar and shake to coat.

• Whisk together the milk and eggs with the rest of the butter.

• Sift the flour into a mixing bowl with a pinch of salt, then stir in the ground almonds and the rest of the sugar.

• Make a well in the middle of the dry ingredients and gradually whisk in the liquid, incorporating all the flour from round the outside until you have a lump-free batter.

• Arrange the kiwi slices in the prepared dishes, then pour in the batter. Bake the clafoutis for 25 minutes or until a skewer inserted in the centre comes out clean.

TASTY LEMON TARTS

MAKES
6

PREPARATION TIME: 1 HOUR
COOKING TIME: 25–30 MINUTES

3 lemons, juiced

175 g / 6 oz / ¾ cup caster (superfine) sugar

2 tsp cornflour (cornstarch)

4 large eggs, beaten

225 ml / 8 fl. oz / ¾ cup double (heavy) cream

FOR THE PASTRY:

150 g / 5 ½ oz / ⅔ cup butter, cubed and chilled

300 g / 10 ½ oz / 1 ½ / 2 cups plain (all-purpose) flour

METHOD

- Rub the butter into the flour until the mixture resembles fine breadcrumbs. Stir in just enough cold water to bring the pastry together into a pliable dough.

- Leave the pastry to chill the fridge for 30 minutes.

- Preheat the oven to 200°C (180°C fan) / 400F / gas 6.

- Roll out the pastry on a floured surface and use it to line 6 individual tart cases. Line them with cling film and fill with baking beans then bake for 10 minutes.

- Remove the pastry cases from the oven and reduce the heat to 160°C (140°C fan) / 325F / gas 3. Stir the lemon juice into the caster sugar and cornflour to dissolve, then whisk in the eggs and cream.

- Strain the mixture into the pastry cases and bake for 15–20 minutes or until just set in the centre.

MINI PEAR TARTE TATIN

MAKES
4

PREPARATION TIME: 10 MINUTES
COOKING TIME: 40 MINUTES

3 tbsp butter, softened and cubed

4 small pears, peeled, halved and cored

4 tbsp soft light brown sugar

100 ml / 3 ½ fl. oz / ½ cup apple juice

100 g / 3 ½ oz / ½ cup hazelnuts
(cobnuts)

300 g / 10 ½ oz all-butter puff pastry

METHOD

• Preheat the oven to 220°C (200°C fan) / 425F / gas 7.

• Melt the butter in a frying pan then fry the pears, cut side down in a single layer, for
5 minutes or until they start to colour.

• Stir the sugar into the apple juice, pour it over the pears then cook until the liquid has
reduced to a syrupy glaze.

• Arrange 2 pears in each hole of a 4-hole Yorkshire pudding tin, then stir the hazelnuts into
the glaze and spoon them over and around the pears.

• Roll out the pastry on a floured surface and cut out 4 circles the same diameter as
the holes. Lay the pastry over the pears and tuck in the edges, then transfer the tin to the
oven and bake for 25 minutes or until the pastry is golden brown and cooked through.

• Using oven gloves, put a large plate or chopping board on top of the tin and turn them both
over in one smooth movement to unmould the tarts.

MINI BLUEBERRY PIES

MAKES
6

PREPARATION TIME: 1 HOUR
COOKING TIME: 25–30 MINUTES

200 g / 7 oz / 1 cup butter, cubed
and chilled

400 g / 14 oz / 2 ⅔ cups plain
(all-purpose) flour

400 g / 14 oz / 2 ⅔ cups blueberries

4 tbsp caster (superfine) sugar

½ tsp cornflour (cornstarch)

1 egg, beaten

METHOD

- Rub the butter into the flour then stir in just enough cold water to make the pastry into a pliable dough. Wrap the dough in cling film and chill for 30 minutes.

- Preheat the oven to 200°C (180°C fan) / 400F / gas 6.

- Roll out half the pastry on a floured surface and cut out 6 circles to line 6 tartlet tins.

- Toss the blueberries with the sugar and cornflour and divide between the 6 pastry cases.

- Roll out the rest of the pastry and cut out 6 circles. Brush the rim of the pastry cases with egg before laying the lids on top then press down firmly round the outside.

- Cut excess pastry into strips and attach them to the top of the pies in a lattice pattern with a little beaten egg.

- Brush the top of the pies with more beaten egg then bake in the oven for 25–30 minutes. Transfer the pies to a wire rack to cool.

TRADITIONAL
PIES

CHEESY COTTAGE PIES

MAKES
6

PREPARATION TIME: 5 MINUTES
COOKING TIME: 1 HOUR 30 MINUTES

2 tbsp olive oil

1 small onion, finely chopped

300 g / 10 ½ oz / 2 cups minced beef

2 cloves of garlic, crushed

250 ml / 9 fl. oz / 1 cup beef stock

2 tsp Worcester sauce

salt and freshly ground black pepper

FOR THE TOPPING:

450 g / 1 lb / 3 ⅔ cups floury potatoes, peeled and cubed

100 ml / 3 ½ fl. oz / ½ cup milk

50 g / 1 ¾ oz / ¼ cup butter

50 g / 1 ¾ oz / ½ cup Cheddar, grated

METHOD

- Heat the oil in a saucepan and fry the onion for 5 minutes. Add the mince and garlic and fry for 5 minutes or until the mince starts to brown.

- Pour in the stock and Worcester sauce and bring to a gentle simmer. Cook for 1 hour, stirring occasionally, until the mince is tender. Season to taste with salt and pepper.

- Meanwhile, cook the potatoes in salted water for 15 minutes, or until they are tender, then drain well. Return the potatoes to the saucepan and add the milk and butter. Mash the potatoes until smooth.

- Preheat the oven to 200°C (180°C fan) / 400F / gas 6. Divide the beef mixture between six ramekin dishes and top with the mashed potato. Use a fork to score a pattern in the top and sprinkle with cheese.

- Bake the pies for 15 minutes or until golden brown and bubbling.

LAMB AND ONION PIE

SERVES
6

PREPARATION TIME: 15 MINUTES
COOKING TIME: 3 HOURS 15 MINUTES

300 ml / 10 ½ fl. oz / 1 ¼ cups lamb stock

600 g/ 1 lb 5 oz lamb shoulder, in large chunks

3 onions, sliced

FOR THE TOPPING:

450 g / 1 lb floury potatoes, peeled and cubed

100 ml / 3 ½ fl. oz / ½ cup milk

50 g / 1 ¾ oz / ¼ cup butter

3 tbsp flat-leaf parsley, leaves only

25 g / 1 oz / ⅓ cup breadcrumbs

METHOD

- Preheat the oven to 150°C (130°C fan) / 300F / gas 2 and bring the stock to the boil.

- Mix the lamb and onions together in a cast iron casserole dish and season well with salt and pepper. Pour over the hot stock then cover the dish and transfer to the oven for 3 hours. 30 minutes before the end of the cooking time, remove the lid so that the onions take on some colour.

- Boil the potatoes in salted water for 12 minutes, or until they are tender, then drain well. Return the potatoes to the saucepan and add the milk, butter and parsley, then mash until smooth.

- Remove the lamb from the oven and increase the temperature to 200°C (180°C fan) / 400F / gas 6.

- Shred the lamb into smaller chunks with 2 forks and stir it back into the onions. Top the lamb with the mashed potato and sprinkle with breadcrumbs, then bake in the oven for 15 minutes or until the top is golden brown.

BEEF AND ALE PIE

SERVES
4

PREPARATION TIME: 25 MINUTES
COOKING TIME: 2 HOURS 40 MINUTES

2 tbsp plain (all-purpose) flour

1 tsp mustard powder

1 kg / 2 lb 3 oz braising steak, cubed

4 tbsp olive oil

1 onion, finely chopped

1 carrot, cubed

3 cloves of garlic, finely chopped

4 sprigs of thyme

600 ml / 1 pint / 2 ½ cups real ale

600 ml / 1 pint / 2 ½ cups good quality beef stock

250 g / 9 oz / 3 cups mushrooms, quartered

250 g / 9 oz all-butter puff pastry

1 egg, beaten

METHOD

- Mix the flour with the mustard powder then season and toss with the beef to coat.

- Heat half of the oil in an oven-proof saucepan and sear the meat in batches until well browned. Remove the beef from the pan, add the rest of the oil and cook the onions, carrots, garlic and thyme for 5 minutes.

- Pour in the beer and boil for 5 minutes then add the stock and return the beef. 30 minutes before end, stir in the mushrooms and season. Bring the casserole to a simmer, cover and cook for 2 hours.

- Preheat the oven to 220°C (200°C fan) / 425F / gas 7.

- Roll out the pastry on a floured surface and cut out a circle a little larger than the saucepan. Brush the top with egg then make the off-cuts into a lattice pattern on top.

- Transfer the pastry to the top of the saucepan, brush with egg, then bake in the oven for 15 minutes.

STEAK, MUSHROOM AND KIDNEY PIE

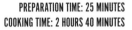

SERVES
4

PREPARATION TIME: 25 MINUTES
COOKING TIME: 2 HOURS 40 MINUTES

4 tbsp olive oil

1 kg / 2 lb 3 oz braising steak, cubed

4 lamb's kidneys, trimmed and cubed

1 onion, finely chopped

3 cloves of garlic, finely chopped

2 bay leaves

600 ml / 1 pint / 2 ½ cups good quality beef stock

250 g / 9 oz / 3 cups mushrooms, quartered

450 g / 1 lb all-butter puff pastry

1 egg, beaten

METHOD

- Heat the oil in an oven-proof saucepan and sear the steak and kidney in batches until well browned.

- Remove the meat from the pan, add the onions, garlic and bay and cook for 5 minutes.

- Pour in the stock, return the beef then simmer for 2 hours.

- 30 minutes before the end of the cooking time, season to taste with salt and pepper and stir in the mushrooms.

- Preheat the oven to 220°C (200°C fan) / 425F / gas 7.

- Roll out half of the pastry and use it to line a large pie dish.

- Ladle the pie filling into the pastry case and brush round the edge with beaten egg.

- Roll out the rest of the pastry and lay it over the pie.

- Scallop the edges and decorate the top with shapes from the off-cuts, then brush with beaten egg and make a hole.

- Bake the pie for 45 minutes or until the pastry is golden.

STEAK AND KIDNEY PIE

SERVES
4

PREPARATION TIME: 2 HOURS 30 MINUTES
COOKING TIME: 45 MINUTES

FOR THE FILLING

2 tbsp vegetable oil or beef dripping

750 g / 1 ⅓ lb / 3 cups stewing beef

200 g / 7 oz / ¾ cup ox kidney, chopped

2 onions, peeled and chopped

1 tbsp tomato purée

1 ½ tbsp plain (all-purpose) flour

2 bay leaves

2 tbsp Worcestershire sauce

450 ml / 15 fl. oz / 1 ¾ cups beef stock

salt and pepper

1 pastry case

METHOD

- Make the filling: Heat the fat in a pan and brown the meat on all sides. Remove with a slotted spoon and add the onions. Cook until softened and golden.

- Stir in the tomato purée, cook out for a few seconds, then tip the meat back into the pan with all its juices. Stir in the flour to make a paste, then the bay leaves, Worcestershire sauce and stock. Season and simmer very gently for 1 ½–2 hours until the meat is tender.

- Tip the filling into the pie dish to come level with the top of the pastry – reserve any excess liquid for gravy. Use a couple of upturned egg cups in the filling to support the lid of the pastry, then carefully place the larger half of pastry onto the pie. Seal the edges by crimping, brush the pastry with beaten egg and make a little hole in the top for the steam to escape.

- Bake in the oven for about 40–45 minutes until the pastry is golden brown.

MUSHROOM PIE

SERVES
4

PREPARATION TIME: 25 MINUTES
COOKING TIME: 30 MINUTES

60 g / 2 oz / ¼ cup butter

1 kg / 2 ¼ lb / 4 ¼ cups field mushrooms, thickly sliced

1 sprig thyme

2 sprigs tarragon

2 cloves garlic, finely sliced

1 tbsp plain (all-purpose) flour

50 ml / 1 ¾ oz / ¼ cup red wine

300 ml / 10 fl. oz / 1 ¼ cups vegetable stock

2 tbsp double (heavy) cream

salt and pepper

500 g / 1 lb ready-made puff pastry

1 egg, beaten

METHOD

• Preheat 200°C (180°C fan) / 400F / gas 6.

• Heat the butter in a large frying pan and cook the mushrooms with the herbs and garlic gently until all the excess liquid has evaporated.

• Add the flour and cook out for 2 minutes, then add the wine and the stock gradually, stirring as you go until smooth. Leave to simmer for 10 minutes until smooth and thick.

• Cut the pastry into two pieces slightly larger than a 20 cm (8 in) pie dish and roll out on a floured surface to about 5 mm thickness.

• Line the pie dish with one circle, then spoon the mushroom filling in, reserving any excess sauce. Lay the second circle on top and crimp the edges together. Brush with beaten egg and make a small slash in the top for the steam to escape.

• Bake on a pre-heated baking sheet for 30 minutes.

CHICKEN HERB PIE

SERVES
6

PREPARATION TIME: 50 MINUTES
COOKING TIME: 30 MINUTES

2 tbsp butter

3–4 chicken thighs, deboned and skinned, diced

1 shallot, finely chopped

5 sprigs thyme and tarragon leaves

1 ½ tbsp plain (all-purpose) flour

300 ml / 10 fl. oz / 1 ¼ cups milk

salt and pepper

1 egg, beaten

FOR THE PASTRY

120 g / 4 oz / ½ cup plain (all-purpose) flour

60 g / 2 oz / ¼ cup butter

pinch of salt

cold water

METHOD

• Sieve the flour and salt into a bowl, then cut the lard and butter into cubes and work into the flour until the mixture resembles breadcrumbs.

• Work in 2 tbsp water and bring the mixture together using enough water to make a smooth ball of dough. Wrap in cling film and chill for 30 minutes.

• Preheat the oven to 200°C (180°C fan) / 400F / gas 6.

• Heat the butter in a pan and fry the chicken until golden. Remove the chicken then sweat the shallot with the herbs. Stir in the flour, then whisk in the milk to make a smooth sauce. Return the chicken to the pan, season and simmer for 10 minutes.

• Tip the chicken into a pie dish. Roll the pastry out on a floured surface to slightly larger than the pie dish and sit on top of the filling.

• Brush with beaten egg, make a hole in the pastry to let the steam escape and bake in the oven for 30 minutes.

MAINS

HAM AND CHEESE TART

SERVES
4

PREPARATION TIME: 10 MINUTES
COOKING TIME: 25 MINUTES

250 g / 9 oz all-butter puff pastry

7 slices goats' cheese

8 thin slices honey-roast ham

METHOD

- Preheat the oven to 220°C (200°C fan) / 425F / gas 7.

- Roll out the pastry on a floured surface and cut out a circle.

- Transfer the pastry to a baking tray and arrange 6 of the goats' cheese slices on top.

- Lay the ham on top and finish with the final slice of cheese then garnish with the rosemary.

- Bake the tart for 25 minutes or until the pastry is golden brown and cooked through.

COTTAGE PIE

SERVES
6

PREPARATION TIME: 5 MINUTES
COOKING TIME: 1 HOUR 30 MINUTES

2 tbsp olive oil

1 small onion, finely chopped

2 cloves of garlic, crushed

450 g / 1 lb / 2 cups minced beef

600 ml / 1 pint / 2 ½ cups beef stock

FOR THE TOPPING:

300 g / 10 ½ oz floury potatoes, peeled and cubed

1 romanesco cauliflower, broken into florets

3 tbsp milk

2 tbsp butter

50 g / 1 ¾ oz / ½ cup Cheddar, grated

METHOD

• Heat the oil in a saucepan and fry the onion for 3 minutes. Add the garlic, cook for 2 minutes, then add the mince.

• Fry the mince until it starts to brown then add the stock and bring to a gentle simmer. Cook for 1 hour, until the mince is tender and the sauce has thickened. Add salt and freshly ground black pepper to taste.

• Meanwhile, boil the potatoes in salted water for 8 minutes, then add the cauliflower florets and cook for a further 5 minutes. Drain well and reserve some cauliflower for decoration then mash the rest with the milk, butter and cheese.

• Preheat the oven to 200°C (180°C fan) / 400F / gas 6.

• Spoon the mince mixture into a large baking dish then top with the mash.

• Stud the top with the reserved cauliflower then bake in the oven for 20 minutes or until golden brown.

DUCK COTTAGE PIE

SERVES
6

PREPARATION TIME: 30 MINUTES
COOKING TIME: 2 HOURS 20 MINUTES

6 duck legs

600 ml / 1 pint / 2 ½ cups duck stock

4 spring onions, finely chopped

2 cloves of garlic, crushed

FOR THE TOPPING:

600 g / 1 lb 5 oz floury potatoes, peeled
and cubed

100 ml / 3 ½ fl. oz / ½ cup milk

50 g / 1 ¾ oz / ¼ cup butter

4 spring onions, chopped

50 g / 1 ¾ oz / ½ cup Cheddar, grated

METHOD

- Put the duck legs in a large saucepan and pour over the stock. Bring to the boil, then cover the pan, turn down the heat and simmer gently for 2 hours.

- Meanwhile, cook the potatoes in salted water for 10 minutes, or until they are tender, then drain well.

- Return the potatoes to the saucepan and add the milk, butter and spring onions. Mash the potatoes.

- Remove the duck legs from the stock and discard the skin. Shred the meat off the bones with a fork and transfer it to a mixing bowl. Add the spring onions and garlic and enough cooking liquid to moisten, then season to taste with salt and pepper.

- Preheat the oven to 200°C (180°C fan) / 400F / gas 6.

- Spoon the duck mixture into a large baking dish then top with the mashed potatoes.

- Sprinkle over the grated cheese and bake in the oven for 20 minutes or until golden brown.

STEAK, POTATO AND TOMATO PIE

SERVES
4

PREPARATION TIME: 1 HOUR
COOKING TIME: 45 MINUTES

450 g / 1 lb potatoes, peeled and sliced

2 tbsp wholegrain mustard

1 large rump steak, diced

4 large ripe tomatoes, peeled, deseeded
and chopped

1 egg, beaten

FOR THE PASTRY:

300 g / 10 ½ oz / 2 cups plain
(all-purpose) flour

150 g / 5 ½ oz / ⅔ cup butter, chilled

METHOD

- Sieve the flour into a bowl then grate in the butter and mix well.

- Mix in enough cold water to form a pliable dough then wrap it in clingfilm and chill for 30 minutes.

- Boil the potatoes in salted water for 5 minutes then drain well.

- Preheat the oven to 190°C (170°C fan) / 375F / gas 5 and butter a 23 cm round pie tin.

- Roll out half of the pastry and use it to line the prepared pie tin.

- Spread the base with mustard then layer up the potatoes with the steak and top with the tomatoes.

- Roll out the rest of the pastry, lay it over the pie and press down round the outside to seal.

- Cut away the excess pastry and crimp the edges with your fingers.

- Cut 2 holes in the lid for the steam to escape then brush the top of the pie with beaten egg.

- Bake the pie for 45 minutes – the pastry should be crisp and golden brown on top and starting to shrink away from the edge of the tin.

CHORIZO AND PARSLEY POTATO-TOPPED PIE

SERVES
6

PREPARATION TIME: 15 MINUTES
COOKING TIME: 15 MINUTES

450 g / 1 lb floury potatoes, peeled and cubed

100 ml / 3 ½ fl. oz / ½ cup milk

50 g / 1 ¾ oz / ¼ cup butter

2 tbsp olive oil

1 onion, finely chopped

2 cloves of garlic, crushed

3 medium tomatoes, diced

250 g / 9 oz chorizo, thinly sliced

a large bunch of parsley, chopped

METHOD

• Preheat the oven to 200°C (180°C fan) / 400F / gas 6.

• Boil the potatoes in salted water for 12 minutes, or until they are tender, then drain well. Return the potatoes to the saucepan and add the milk and butter, then mash until smooth.

• While the potatoes are cooking, heat the oil in a frying pan and fry the onion and garlic for 5 minutes. Add the tomatoes and cook for 2 more minutes, then combine with the chorizo and parsley.

• Spoon the mixture into a baking dish and top with the mashed potato.

• Level the top with a spatula, then bake in the oven for 15 minutes or until the potato is golden brown.

LAMB AND HAZELNUT POTATO-TOPPED PIES

MAKES
6

PREPARATION TIME: 10 MINUTES
COOKING TIME: 2 HOURS 30 MINUTES

2 tbsp olive oil

1 small onion, finely chopped

1 carrot, grated

2 cloves of garlic, crushed

1 tsp ground cumin

450 g/ 1 lb lamb shoulder, cubed

600 ml / 1 pint / 2 ½ cups lamb stock

salad leaves to garnish

FOR THE TOPPING:

450 g / 1 lb floury potatoes, peeled and cubed

100 ml / 3 ½ fl. oz / ½ cup milk

50 g / 1 ¾ oz / ¼ cup butter

50 g / 1 ¾ oz / ⅓ cup hazelnuts (cobnuts), chopped

METHOD

- Heat the oil in a saucepan and fry the onion, garlic, carrot and cumin for 3 minutes. Add the lamb shoulder and fry for 2 minutes then add the stock.

- Lay greaseproof paper on top of the meat and cover the pan with a lid then simmer gently for 2 hours.

- Preheat the oven to 200°C (180°C fan) / 400F / gas 6.

- Cook the potatoes in salted water for 10 minutes, then drain well. Return the potatoes to the saucepan and add the milk and butter, then mash.

- Shred the lamb with 2 forks and season to taste with salt and pepper. Arrange 6 metal ring moulds on a baking tray and half-fill each one with the lamb.

- Top the lamb with the mashed potato and sprinkle with hazelnuts, then bake in the oven for 15 minutes or until the tops are golden brown.

- Unmould the pies onto warm plates and garnish with salad leaves.

SHEPHERD'S PIE

SERVES
6

PREPARATION TIME: 10 MINUTES
COOKING TIME: 2 HOURS 45 MINUTES

4 tbsp olive oil

450 g / 1 lb / 3 cups boneless lamb shoulder, diced

1 onion, finely chopped

1 carrot, finely chopped

1 celery stick, finely chopped

2 cloves of garlic, crushed

1 tsp dried oregano

1 tbsp tomato purée

250 ml / 9 fl. oz / 1 cup lamb stock

FOR THE TOPPING:

450 g / 1 lb / 3 ⅔ cups floury potatoes, peeled and cubed

100 ml / 3 ½ fl. oz / ½ cup milk

100 g / 3 ½ oz / ½ cup butter

1 tbsp flat-leaf parsley, finely chopped

METHOD

- Heat half the oil in a sauté pan and sear the lamb in batches on all sides. Transfer the lamb to a bowl then add the rest of the oil to the pan and fry the onion, carrot and celery for 10 minutes. Add the garlic and fry for 2 minutes, then stir in the oregano and tomato purée.

- Pour in the stock, return the lamb and bring to a gentle simmer. Cover and cook over a low heat for 2 hours, stirring occasionally, until the lamb is very tender. Season to taste with salt and pepper.

- Towards the end of the cooking time, boil the potatoes in salted water for 15 minutes, or until tender, then drain well. Return the potatoes to the saucepan and add the milk and butter. Mash the potatoes until smooth.

- Preheat the oven to 200°C (180°C fan) / 400F / gas 6. Spoon the lamb mixture into a baking dish and top with the mashed potato.

- Bake for 25 minutes or until golden brown and bubbling then sprinkle with parsley before serving.

BEEF AND COURGETTE POTATO-TOPPED PIE

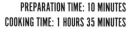

SERVES
6

PREPARATION TIME: 10 MINUTES
COOKING TIME: 1 HOURS 35 MINUTES

2 tbsp olive oil

1 small onion, finely chopped

2 courgettes (zucchini), halved and sliced

2 cloves of garlic, crushed

1 tbsp tomato purée

450 g / 1 lb / 2 cups minced beef

300 ml / 10 fl. oz / 1 ¼ cups beef stock

FOR THE TOPPING:

800 g / 1 lb 12 oz floury potatoes, peeled and cubed

100 ml / 3 ½ fl. oz / ½ cup milk

100 g / 3 ½ oz / ½ cup butter

2 tbsp Parmesan, finely grated

50 g / 1 ¾ oz / ⅓ cup panko breadcrumbs

METHOD

• Heat the oil in a saucepan and fry the onion, courgette and garlic for 3 minutes. Add the mince and fry for 2 minutes then stir in the tomato purée.

• Add the stock and bring to a simmer then cover the pan with a lid and simmer very gently for 1 hour.

• Preheat the oven to 200°C (180°C fan) / 400F / gas 6.

• Cook the potatoes in salted water for 10 minutes, or until they are tender, then drain well. Return the potatoes to the saucepan and add the milk and butter, then mash until smooth.

• Spoon the mince into a baking dish and spread it out in an even layer.

• Top with the mashed potato and smooth it over.

• Sprinkle the top of the pie with Parmesan and breadcrumbs, then bake in the oven for 25 minutes or until the top is golden brown.

SAUSAGEMEAT PIE

SERVES
4

2 tbsp olive oil

1 small onion, finely chopped

2 cloves of garlic, crushed

450 g / 1 lb / 2 cups pork sausagemeat

400 ml / 14 fl. oz / 1 ⅔ cups beef stock

FOR THE TOPPING:

450 g / 1 lb floury potatoes, peeled and cubed

100 ml / 3 ½ fl. oz / ½ cup milk

50 g / 1 ¾ oz / ¼ cup butter

flat-leaf parsley to garnish

METHOD

- Fry the onion for 3 minutes, stirring occasionally.

- Add the garlic and cook for 2 minutes, then add the sausagemeat, breaking it up with the spoon.

- Fry the sausagemeat until it starts to brown then add the stock and bring to a gentle simmer. Cook for 30 minutes, until the meat is tender. Add salt and ground black pepper to taste.

- Meanwhile, cook the potatoes in salted water for 10 minutes, or until they are tender, then drain well.

- Return the potatoes to the saucepan and add the milk and butter. Mash the potatoes until smooth.

- Preheat the oven to 200°C (180°C fan) / 400F / gas 6. Spoon the mince mixture into a large baking dish then top with the mashed potatoes.

- Level the top then bake in the oven for 20 minutes or until golden brown. Garnish with parsley.

CHICKEN AND ALMOND PASTILLA

MAKES
6

PREPARATION TIME: 25 MINUTES
COOKING TIME: 25–30 MINUTES

1 onion, finely chopped

2 tbsp olive oil

2 chicken breasts, finely chopped

2 cloves garlic, crushed

1 lemon, zest finely grated

100 g / 3 ½ oz / ¾ cup blanched almonds, chopped

3 tbsp coriander (cilantro) leaves, chopped

225 g / 8 oz filo pastry

100 g / 3 ½ oz / ½ cup butter, melted

icing (confectioners') sugar to dust

METHOD

• Preheat the oven to 180°C (160°C fan) / 350F / gas 4 and grease a large baking tray.

• Fry the onion for 5 minutes then add the chicken and garlic and stir-fry for 3 minutes. Turn off the heat and stir in the lemon zest, almonds and coriander. Season with salt and pepper and leave to cool a little.

• Brush the pastry sheets with butter and layer them to create 6 separate stacks.

• Divide the chicken mixture between the filo stacks and fold in the edges.

• Turn the parcels over and transfer to the baking tray. Brush with a little extra butter then bake for 25–30 minutes or until the pastry is crisp and golden.

• Dust the pastillas with icing sugar before serving.

• To create the char marks, heat up a skewer with a blow torch or gas hob and burn lines in the icing sugar.

TOMATO TARTS

MAKES
6-8

PREPARATION TIME: 30 MINUTES
COOKING TIME: 12 MINUTES

1 pack ready-rolled puff pastry

1 tbsp butter

1 onion, peeled and finely chopped

2 cloves of garlic, finely chopped

200ml / 6 ½ fl oz / ¾ cup passata

small handful oregano leaves

salt and pepper

1–2 ripe tomatoes, thickly sliced

8 black olives, stoned and halved

8 anchovy fillets

METHOD

- Preheat the oven to 200°C (180°C fan) / 400F / gas 6.

- Cut out pastry circles about 7cm in diameter from the sheet. You should make between 6 and 8. Place on a greased baking sheet and bake in the oven for 12 minutes until crisp and golden.

- When cooked, push the middle of each pastry circle down a little with a spoon to create a space for the filling.

- Heat the butter in a pan and cook the onion and garlic until golden. Add the passata and oregano and heat briskly until reduced and thick. Adjust the seasoning.

- Spoon into the middle of the pastry cases, then top with a slice of fresh tomato.

- Place the anchovy and 2 olive halves on top and grill until bubbling.

- Leave to cool before eating.

ITALIAN VEGETABLE TART

SERVES
6

PREPARATION TIME: 40 MINUTES
COOKING TIME: 35–40 MINUTES

2 x 375 g packs ready-rolled shortcrust pastry

1 egg, beaten

FOR THE FILLING

olive oil

1 onion, peeled and finely chopped

2 cloves of garlic, finely sliced

1 aubergine (eggplant), cut into thin slices

2 courgettes (zucchini), cut into thin slices

1 jar roasted red peppers

2 eggs, beaten

275 ml / 10 fl oz / 1 cup double (heavy) cream

salt and pepper

METHOD

- Preheat the oven to 180°C (160°C fan) / 350F / gas 4.

- Roll out 1 pastry sheet and use to line a pie dish.

- Heat the oil in a pan and cook the onion and garlic until golden. Move from the pan to a bowl using a slotted spoon.

- Add the aubergine (eggplant) and a drop of oil and cook until tender, taking care to try to keep the slices intact. Place them on kitchen paper and repeat with the courgette slices.

- Layer the vegetables with the peppers in the base of the pie dish, alternating the layers.

- Whisk together the eggs and cream, season and pour over the vegetables.

- Roll out the remaining pastry sheet and cut into 1 cm wide strips. Use them to form a lattice on top of the pie.

- Bake in the oven for around 35–40 minutes until the pastry is golden. Serve warm.

DESSERTS

APPLE AND VANILLA PIE

SERVES
6-8

PREPARATION TIME: 45 MINUTES
COOKING TIME: 35-45 MINUTES

125 g / 4 ½ oz / ½ cup caster (superfine) sugar

2 tbsp plain (all-purpose) flour

1 vanilla pod, seeds only

900 g / 2 lb bramley apples, peeled and chopped

1 egg, beaten

FOR THE PASTRY

300 g / 11 oz / 2 cups plain (all-purpose) flour

150 g / 5 ½ oz / ⅔ cup butter, chilled

METHOD

- Sieve the flour into a mixing bowl. Dip the chilled butter in the flour then grate it into the bowl and mix evenly.

- Add enough cold water to bring it together into a pliable dough then chill for 30 minutes.

- Preheat the oven to 190°C (170°C fan) / 375F / gas 5 and butter a 23 cm round pie tin.

- Mix the sugar, flour and vanilla seeds together then add the apples and mix together.

- Roll out half the pastry on a floured surface and use it to line the pie tin.

- Pack the apples into the pastry case and brush around the top of the pastry with beaten egg.

- Roll out the other half of the pastry and lay it over the apples. Press down round the outside to seal.

- Crimp the edges and trim away any excess pastry.

- Make a couple of holes in the top with a knife and brush with beaten egg then bake for 35–45 minutes – the pastry should be crisp and golden brown on top and starting to shrink away from the edge of the tin.

CHOCOLATE PEAR TART

SERVES
8

PREPARATION TIME: 40 MINUTES
COOKING TIME: 35 MINUTES

110 g / 4 oz / ½ cup butter, cubed and chilled

225 g / 8 oz / 1 ½ cups plain (all-purpose) flour

200 g / 7 oz dark chocolate (minimum 60% cocoa solids), chopped

4 pears, cored and sliced

2 tbsp desiccated coconut

METHOD

- Rub the butter into the flour then add just enough cold water to bind the mixture into a pliable dough.

- Roll out the pastry on a floured surface and use it to line a 23 cm (9 in) round tart case. Leave the pastry to chill the fridge for 30 minutes.

- Preheat the oven to 200°C (180°C fan) / 400F / gas 6.

- Line the pastry case with cling film and fill it with baking beans, then bake for 15 minutes.

- Remove the cling film and baking beans and fill the case with chopped chocolate, then arrange the pear slices on top.

- Bake for 15–20 minutes or until the pears are soft and golden.

- Sprinkle the tart with desiccated coconut just before serving.

MANGO TARTE TATIN

SERVES
8

PREPARATION TIME: 10 MINUTES
COOKING TIME: 25 MINUTES

3 tbsp butter, softened and cubed

4 tbsp soft light brown sugar

2 mangos, peeled, stoned and sliced

250 g / 9 oz all-butter puff pastry

METHOD

- Preheat the oven to 220°C (200°C fan) / 425F / gas 7.

- Dot the butter over the base of a large ovenproof frying pan and sprinkle with sugar, then arrange the mango on top.

- Roll out the pastry on a floured surface and cut out a circle the same size as the frying pan.

- Lay the pastry over the fruit and tuck in the edges, then transfer the pan to the oven and bake for 25 minutes or until the pastry is golden brown and cooked through.

- Using oven gloves, put a large plate on top of the frying pan and turn them both over in one smooth movement to unmould the tart.

MIRABELLE CLAFOUTIS

SERVES
6

PREPARATION TIME: 15 MINUTES
COOKING TIME: 35-45 MINUTES

75 g / 2 ½ oz / ⅓ cup caster (superfine) sugar

75 g / 2 ½ oz / ⅓ cup butter

300 ml / 10 ½ fl. oz / 1 ¼ cups whole milk

2 large eggs

50 g / 1 ¾ oz / ⅓ cup plain (all-purpose) flour

2 tbsp ground almonds

300 g / 10 ½ oz / 2 cups mirabelle plums

demerara sugar for sprinkling

METHOD

• Preheat the oven to 190°C (170°C fan) / 375F / gas 5.

• Melt the butter in a saucepan and cook over a low heat until it starts to smell nutty.

• Brush a little of the butter around the inside of a baking dish then add a spoonful of the caster sugar and shake to coat.

• Whisk together the milk and eggs with the rest of the butter.

• Sift the flour into a mixing bowl with a pinch of salt, then stir in the ground almonds and the rest of the sugar.

• Make a well in the middle of the dry ingredients and gradually whisk in the liquid, incorporating all the flour from round the outside until you have a lump-free batter.

• Arrange the mirabelles in the prepared baking dish, pour over the batter and sprinkle with demerara sugar.

• Bake the clafoutis for 35–45 minutes or until a skewer inserted in the centre comes out clean.

PEACH AND PISTACHIO CLAFOUTIS

SERVES
6

PREPARATION TIME: 10 MINUTES
COOKING TIME: 35-45 MINUTES

75 g / 2 ½ oz / ⅓ cup caster (superfine) sugar

75 g / 2 ½ oz / ⅓ cup butter

300 ml / 10 ½ fl. oz / 1 ¼ cups whole milk

2 large eggs

50 g / 1 ¾ oz / ⅓ cup plain (all-purpose) flour

2 peaches, stoned and sliced

3 tbsp pistachio nuts, chopped

METHOD

• Preheat the oven to 190°C (170°C fan) / 375F / gas 5.

• Melt the butter in a saucepan and cook over a low heat until it starts to smell nutty.

• Brush a little of the butter around the inside of a baking dish then add a spoonful of caster sugar and shake to coat.

• Whisk together the milk and eggs with the rest of the butter.

• Sift the flour into a mixing bowl with a pinch of salt, then stir in the rest of the sugar.

• Make a well in the middle of the dry ingredients and gradually whisk in the liquid, incorporating all the flour from round the outside until you have a lump-free batter.

• Arrange the peaches in the prepared baking dish, pour over the batter and sprinkle with chopped pistachios.

• Bake the clafoutis for 35–45 minutes or until a skewer inserted in the centre comes out clean.

PEAR TARTE TATIN

SERVES 8

PREPARATION TIME: 10 MINUTES
COOKING TIME: 40 MINUTES

3 tbsp butter, softened and cubed

5 small pears, peeled, quartered and cored

4 tbsp soft light brown sugar

100 ml / 3 ½ fl. oz / ½ cup apple juice

300 g / 10 ½ oz all-butter puff pastry

METHOD

- Preheat the oven to 220°C (200°C fan) / 425F / gas 7.

- Melt the butter in a large frying pan then fry the pears, in a single layer, for 5 minutes or until they start to colour.

- Stir the sugar into the apple juice and pour it over the pears then cook until the liquid has reduced to a syrupy glaze.

- Arrange the pears in a small oven-proof prying pan and spoon over the cooking liquid.

- Roll out the pastry on a floured surface and cut out a circle the same diameter as the pan.

- Lay the pastry over the pears and tuck in the edges, then transfer the tin to the oven and bake for 25 minutes or until the pastry is golden brown and cooked through.

- Using oven gloves, put a large plate on top of the pan and turn them both over in one smooth movement to unmould the tart.

APRICOT JAM TART

SERVES
8

PREPARATION TIME: 40 MINUTES
COOKING TIME: 35 MINUTES

100 g / 3 ½ oz / ½ cup butter, cubed and chilled

200 g / 7 oz / 1 ⅓ cups plain (all-purpose) flour

450 g / 1 lb / 1 ¼ cups apricot jam

1 egg, beaten

physalis to garnish

METHOD

- Preheat the oven to 200°C (180°C fan) / 400F / gas 6.

- Rub the butter into the flour until the mixture resembles fine breadcrumbs.

- Stir in just enough cold water to bring the pastry together into a pliable dough then chill for 30 minutes.

- Roll out the pastry on a floured surface and use it to line a 23 cm round tart case, then trim off and reserve the excess pastry.

- Spoon the jam into the pastry case and level the top. Roll out the pastry trimmings and cut into 1 cm slices. Arrange them in a lattice pattern on top of the tart then seal the edges and brush the top with beaten egg.

- Bake for 25–30 minutes or until the pastry is cooked through underneath then garnish with physalis.

LIME MERINGUE PIE

**SERVES
8**

PREPARATION TIME: 10 MINUTES
COOKING TIME: 25 MINUTES

2 tsp cornflour (cornstarch)

8 limes, juiced and zest finely grated

4 large eggs, beaten

225 g / 8 oz / 1 cup butter

175 g / 6 oz / ¾ cup caster
(superfine) sugar

FOR THE BASE:

200 g / 7 oz ginger nut biscuits, crushed

3 tbsp butter, melted

FOR THE MERINGUE:

4 large egg whites

100g / 3 ½ oz / ½ cup caster (superfine) sugar

slices of lime to garnish

METHOD

- Preheat the oven to 200°C (180°C fan) / 390F / gas 6.

- Mix the biscuit crumbs with the butter and press into an even layer in the bottom of a 23 cm round tart case.

- Bake the biscuit layer for 5 minutes or until firm.

- Meanwhile, dissolve the cornflour in the lime juice and put it in a saucepan with the rest of the ingredients.

- Stir constantly over a medium heat to melt the butter and dissolve the sugar. Bring to a gentle simmer then pour it onto the biscuit base.

- Whisk the egg whites until stiff, then gradually add the sugar and whisk until the mixture is thick and shiny.

- Spoon the meringue on top of the lime curd, then bake for 10 minutes or until golden brown on top.

- Cut the pie into slices and garnish with lime.

ORANGE MERINGUE PIE

SERVES
8

PREPARATION TIME: 55 MINUTES
COOKING TIME: 25-30 MINUTES

2 tsp cornflour (cornstarch)

2 oranges, juiced and zest finely grated

2 lemons, juiced and zest finely grated

4 large eggs, beaten

225 g / 8 oz / 1 cup butter

175 g / 6 oz / ¾ cup caster
(superfine) sugar

FOR THE PASTRY:

100 g / 3 ½ oz / ½ cup butter, cubed

200 g / 7 oz / 1 ⅓ cups plain (all-purpose) flour

FOR THE MERINGUE:

4 large egg whites

100g / 3 ½ oz / ½ cup caster (superfine) sugar

METHOD

• Preheat the oven to 200°C (180°C fan) / 390F/ gas 6.

• Rub butter into the flour and add cold water to bind.

• Chill for 30 minutes then roll out on a floured surface.

• Use the pastry to line a 24 cm loose-bottomed tart tin and prick it with a fork.

• Line the pastry with cling film and fill with baking beans or rice then bake for 10 minutes.

• Remove the cling film and beans and cook for 8 minutes.

• Dissolve the cornflour in the orange and lemon juice and put it in a pan with the rest of the ingredients.

• Stir constantly over a medium heat to melt the butter and dissolve the sugar. Pour it into the pastry case.

• Whisk the egg whites until stiff, then gradually add the sugar and whisk until the mixture is thick and shiny.

• Spoon the meringue on top of the orange mixture, leaving a border round the edge and make peaks. Bake for 10 minutes.

RASPBERRY AND VIOLET CUSTARD TART

SERVES
8

PREPARATION TIME: 40 MINUTES
COOKING TIME: 55 MINUTES

100 g / 3 ½ oz / ½ cup butter, cubed

200 g / 7 oz / 1 ⅓ cups plain (all-purpose) flour

4 large egg yolks

75 g / 2 ½ oz / ⅓ cup caster (superfine) sugar

1 tsp vanilla extract

2 tsp cornflour (cornstarch)

450 ml / 16 fl. oz / 1 ¾ cups milk

50 g / 1 ¾ oz / ⅔ cup crystallised violets, plus
extra for sprinkling

250 g / 9 oz / 1 ⅔ cups raspberries

METHOD

• Preheat the oven to 200°C (180°C fan) / 390 F / gas 6.

• Rub butter into the flour and add cold water to bind.

• Chill for 30 minutes then roll out on a floured surface. Use the pastry to line a 23 cm
round tart case.

• Prick the pastry with a fork, line with cling film and fill with baking beans or rice.

• Bake for 10 minutes then remove the cling film and baking beans and cook for a further
8 minutes to crisp.

• Reduce oven temperature to 160°C (140°C fan) / 325F / gas 3.

• Whisk together the egg yolks, sugar, vanilla, cornflour and milk and strain it through a
sieve. Stir in the crystallised violets and pour it into the pastry case.

• Bake the tart for 35 minutes or until the custard is just set in the centre.

• Leave to cool completely then arrange the raspberries on top and sprinkle with a few more
crystallised violets.

PEAR AND CHOCOLATE TART

SERVES
8

PREPARATION TIME: 40 MINUTES
COOKING TIME: 55 MINUTES

100 g / 3 ½ oz / ½ cup butter, cubed

200 g / 7 oz / 1 ⅓ cups plain (all-purpose) flour

400 g / 14 oz canned pear halves, drained and chopped

4 large egg yolks

75 g / 2 ½ oz / ⅓ cup caster (superfine) sugar

1 tsp vanilla extract

2 tsp cornflour (cornstarch)

2 tbsp unsweetened cocoa powder

450 ml / 16 fl. oz / 1 ¾ cups milk

edible flowers to garnish

METHOD

- Preheat the oven to 200°C (180°C fan) / 400F / gas 6.

- Rub the butter into the flour and add just enough cold water to bind.

- Chill for 30 minutes then roll out on a floured surface. Use the pastry to line a 23 cm round tart case.

- Prick the pastry with a fork, line with cling film and fill with baking beans or rice.

- Bake for 10 minutes then remove the cling film and baking beans and cook for a further 8 minutes to crisp.

- Reduce the oven temperature to 160°C (140°C fan) / 325F / gas 3.

- Arrange the chopped pears in the pastry case.

- Whisk together the egg yolks, sugar, vanilla, cornflour, cocoa and milk and strain it through a sieve onto the pears.

- Bake the tart for 35 minutes or until the custard is just set in the centre.

- Leave to cool completely then garnish with edible flowers.

APPLE, COCONUT AND PISTACHIO PIE

SERVES
6

PREPARATION TIME: 45 MINUTES
COOKING TIME: 45 MINUTES

125 g / 4 ½ oz / ½ cup caster (superfine) sugar

3 tbsp desiccated coconut

800 g / 12 oz bramley apples, peeled,
cored and diced

2 tbsp sultanas

1 egg, beaten

50 g / 1 ¾ oz / ½ cup sweetened shredded coconut

25 g / 1 oz / ¼ cup pistachio nuts, finely chopped

FOR THE PASTRY:

300 g / 10 ½ oz / 2 cups plain (all-purpose) flour

150 g / 5 ½ oz / ⅔ cup butter, chilled

METHOD

- Sieve the flour into a bowl then grate in the butter and mix well.

- Mix in enough cold water to form a pliable dough then wrap it in cling film and chill for 30 minutes.

- Preheat the oven to 190°C (170°C fan) / 375F / gas 5 and butter a 23 cm round pie tin.

- Mix the sugar and coconut together in a bowl then toss with the apples and sultanas.

- Roll out half of the pastry and use it to line the prepared pie tin.

- Pack the apples into the pastry case and wet the rim with water.

- Roll out the rest of the pastry, lay it over the apples and press down round the outside to seal.

- Cut away the excess pastry and crimp the edges with your fingers.

- Cut 2 holes in the lid for the steam to escape then bake for 45 minutes or until the pastry is cooked through underneath.

- Sprinkle the top with the shredded coconut and pistachio nuts.

FRUITY FRANGIPANE TARTS

MAKES
4

PREPARATION TIME: 50 MINUTES
COOKING TIME: 30 MINUTES

110 g / 4 oz / ½ cup butter, cubed and chilled

225 g / 8 oz / 1 ½ cups plain (all-purpose) flour

FOR THE FILLING:

55 g / 2 oz / ½ cup ground almonds

55 g / 2 oz / ¼ cup caster (superfine) sugar

55 g / 2 oz / ¼ cup butter, softened

1 large egg

1 tsp almond extract

200 g / 7 oz / 1 ⅓ cups blueberries, blackcurrants or raspberries

METHOD

- Rub the butter into the flour then add just enough cold water to bind the mixture together into a pliable dough.

- Roll out the pastry on a floured surface and use it to line four individual tart cases. Leave the pastry to chill the fridge for 30 minutes.

- Preheat the oven to 200°C (180°C fan) / 400F / gas 6.

- Line the pastry cases with cling film and fill them with baking beans or rice, then bake for 10 minutes.

- To make the frangipane, combine the ground almonds, sugar, butter, egg and almond extract in a bowl and whisk together for 2 minutes or until smooth.

- When the tart cases are ready, remove the cling film and baking beans and fill each one with frangipane. Top with your chosen berries, pressing them down into the mixture.

- Bake for 20 minutes or until a skewer inserted comes out clean. Serve hot or cold.

CHOCOLATE CUSTARD TART

SERVES
8

PREPARATION TIME: 40 MINUTES
COOKING TIME: 55 MINUTES

100 g / 3 ½ oz / ½ cup butter, cubed

200 g / 7 oz / 1 ⅓ cups plain (all-purpose) flour

4 large egg yolks

75 g / 2 ½ oz / ⅓ cup caster (superfine) sugar

1 tsp vanilla extract

2 tsp cornflour (cornstarch)

2 tbsp unsweetened cocoa powder

450 ml / 16 fl. oz / 1 ¾ cups milk

icing (confectioners') sugar for dusting

METHOD

• Preheat the oven to 200°C (180°C fan) / 390F / gas 6.

• Rub butter into the flour and add cold water to bind.

• Chill for 30 minutes then roll out on a floured surface. Use the pastry to line a 23 cm round tart case.

• Prick the pastry with a fork, line with cling film and fill with baking beans or rice.

• Bake for 10 minutes then remove the clingfilm and baking beans and cook for a further 8 minutes to crisp.

• Reduce the oven temperature to 160°C (140°C fan) / 325F / gas 3.

• Whisk together the egg yolks, sugar, vanilla, cornflour, cocoa and milk and strain it through a sieve into the pastry case.

• Bake the tart for 35 minutes.

• Leave to cool completely then hold a stencil over the tart and dust with icing sugar.

PUMPKIN PIE

SERVES 10

PREPARATION TIME: 55 MINUTES
COOKING TIME: 1 HOUR 10 MINUTES

600 g / 1 lb 5 oz pumpkin or butternut squash,
peeled, deseeded and cubed

2 large eggs

150 ml / 5 ½ fl. oz / ⅔ cup maple syrup

150 ml / 5 ½ fl. oz / ⅔ evaporated milk

1 tsp mixed spice

1 pastry case, sweet

METHOD

• Preheat the oven to 200°C (180°C fan) / 400F / gas 6.

• Put the pumpkin in a roasting tin and cover with foil then bake for 30 minutes.

• Drain the pumpkin of any excess liquid then purée it in a food processor.

• Add the eggs, maple syrup, evaporated milk and spice and pulse until smoothly combined.

• Reduce the oven temperature to 180°C (160°C fan) / 350F / gas 4.

• Pour the pumpkin mixture into the pastry case and bake for 30–40 minutes or until just set in the centre.

• Leave to cool completely before slicing.

PLUM TARTE TATIN

SERVES
8

PREPARATION TIME: 10 MINUTES
COOKING TIME: 25 MINUTES

3 tbsp butter, softened and cubed

4 tbsp soft light brown sugar

4 pears, peeled, cored and quartered

12 small plums, stoned

6 mirabelles, stoned

250 g / 9 oz all-butter puff pastry

METHOD

- Preheat the oven to 220°C (200°C fan) / 425F / gas 7.

- Dot the butter over the base of a large ovenproof frying pan and sprinkle with sugar.

- Arrange the pears round the outside of the pan, followed by a ring of plums and the mirabelles in the centre.

- Roll out the pastry on a floured surface and cut out a circle the same size as the frying pan.

- Lay the pastry over the fruit and tuck in the edges, then transfer the pan to the oven and bake for 25 minutes or until the pastry is golden brown and cooked through.

- Using oven gloves, put a large plate on top of the frying pan and turn them both over in one smooth movement to unmould the tart.

APPLE PIE

SERVES
6-8

PREPARATION TIME: 45 MINUTES
COOKING TIME: 35–45 MINUTES

125 g / 4 ½ oz / ½ cup caster (superfine) sugar

2 tbsp plain (all-purpose) flour

½ tsp ground cinnamon

800 g / 12 oz bramley apples, peeled, cored and cut into chunks

1 egg, beaten

FOR THE PASTRY:

300 g / 10 ½ oz / 2 cups plain (all-purpose) flour

150 g / 5 ½ oz / ⅔ cup butter, chilled

METHOD

- Sieve the flour into a bowl then grate in the butter and mix well.

- Mix in enough cold water to form a pliable dough then wrap it in cling film and chill for 30 minutes.

- Preheat the oven to 190°C (170°C fan) / 375F / gas 5 and butter a 23 cm round pie tin.

- Mix the sugar, flour and cinnamon together in a bowl then toss with the apples.

- Roll out half of the pastry and use it to line the prepared pie tin.

- Pack the apples into the pastry case and brush around the rim with beaten egg.

- Roll out the rest of the pastry, lay it over the apples and press down round the outside to seal. Cut away the excess pastry and crimp the edges with your fingers.

- Cut 2 holes in the lid for the steam to escape then brush the top of the pie with beaten egg.

- Bake the pie for 35–45 minutes – the pastry should be crisp and golden brown on top and starting to shrink away from the edge of the tin.

CUSTARD TART

SERVES
8

PREPARATION TIME: 40 MINUTES
COOKING TIME: 55 MINUTES

100 g / 3 ½ oz / ½ cup butter, cubed

200 g / 7 oz / 1 ⅓ cups plain (all-purpose) flour

4 large egg yolks

75 g / 2 ½ oz / ⅓ cup caster (superfine) sugar

1 tsp vanilla extract

2 tsp cornflour (cornstarch)

450 ml / 16 fl. oz / 1 ¾ cups milk

METHOD

• Preheat the oven to 200°C (180°C fan) / 390F/ gas 6.

• Rub the butter into the flour and add just enough cold water to bind.

• Chill for 30 minutes then roll out on a floured surface. Use the pastry to line a 23 cm round tart case.

• Prick the pastry with a fork, line with cling film and fill with baking beans or rice.

• Bake for 10 minutes then remove the cling film and baking beans and cook for a further 8 minutes to crisp.

• Reduce the oven temperature to 160°C (140°C fan) / 325F / gas 3.

• Whisk together the egg yolks, sugar, vanilla, cornflour and milk and strain it through a sieve into the pastry case.

• Bake the tart for 35 minutes or until the custard is just set in the centre.

• Leave to cool completely before slicing.

PECAN PIE

SERVES
8

PREPARATION TIME: 40 MINUTES
COOKING TIME: 45 MINUTES

200 g / 7 oz / 1 ¼ cup dark brown sugar

100 g / 3 ½ oz / ⅓ cup golden syrup

100 g / 3 ½ oz / ½ cup butter

1 tsp vanilla extract

3 large eggs, beaten

3 tbsp plain (all-purpose) flour

1 tsp mixed spice

300 g / 10 ½ oz / 1 ½ cups pecan halves

softly whipped cream to serve

FOR THE PASTRY:

150 g / 5 ½ / ⅔ cup butter, cubed and chilled

300 g / 10 ½ oz / 2 cups plain (all-purpose) flour

METHOD

- Sieve the flour into a bowl then grate in the butter and mix well.

- Mix in enough cold water to form a pliable dough then wrap it in cling film and chill for 30 minutes.

- Preheat the oven to 190°C (170°C fan) / 375F / gas 5 and butter a 23 cm round pie tin.

- Mix the sugar, flour and cinnamon together in a bowl then toss with the apples.

- Roll out half of the pastry and use it to line the prepared pie tin.

- Pack the apples into the pastry case and brush around the rim with beaten egg.

- Roll out the rest of the pastry, lay it over the apples and press down round the outside to seal. Cut away the excess pastry and crimp the edges with your fingers.

- Cut 2 holes in the lid for the steam to escape then brush the top of the pie with beaten egg.

- Bake the pie for 35–45 minutes – the pastry should be crisp and golden brown on top and starting to shrink away from the edge of the tin.

BANOFFEE PIE

SERVES
12

PREPARATION TIME: 45 MINUTES
COOKING TIME: 3 HOURS 20 MINUTES

400 g / 14 oz can of condensed milk

110 g / 4 oz / ½ cup butter, cubed and chilled

225 g / 8 oz / 1 ½ cups plain (all-purpose) flour

3 bananas, chopped

300 ml / 10 ½ fl. oz / 1 ¼ cups double (heavy) cream

25 g / 1 oz dark chocolate

METHOD

• Put the unopened can of condensed milk in a saucepan of water and simmer for 3 hours, adding more water as necessary to ensure it doesn't boil dry. Leave to cool completely.

• Rub the butter into the flour then add just enough cold water to bind the mixture together into a pliable dough.

• Roll out the pastry on a floured surface and use it to line a 23 cm (9 in) round tart case.

• Leave the pastry to chill for 30 minutes.

• Preheat the oven to 200°C (180°C fan) / 400F / gas 6.

• Line the pastry case with cling film and fill it with baking beans, then bake for 15 minutes.

• Remove the cling film and beans and return to the oven until golden brown and crisp. Leave to cool.

• Open the can of condensed milk and beat the caramel until smooth then stir in the banana.

• Spoon the mixture into the pastry case and level the top.

• Whip the cream until it holds its shape, then spoon on top of the caramel layer.

• Grate over the chocolate before serving.

SPEEDY PLUM TART

SERVES
4

PREPARATION TIME: 10 MINUTES
COOKING TIME: 25 MINUTES

250 g / 9 oz all-butter puff pastry

1 egg, beaten

6 plums, stoned and thinly sliced

2 tbsp caster (superfine) sugar

METHOD

• Preheat the oven to 220°C (200°C fan) / 425F / gas 7.

• Roll out the pastry on a floured surface into a rectangle.

• Transfer the pastry to a baking sheet and brush with beaten egg then arrange the sliced plums on top.

• Sprinkle with sugar, then transfer the tray to the oven and bake for 25 minutes or until the pastry is golden brown and cooked through.

INDEX